ENGINEER DEPARTMENT, UNITED STATES ARMY.

REPORT

ON THE

EFFECTS OF THE SEA-WATER AND EXPOSURE

UPON THE

IRON-PILE SHAFTS

OF

THE BRANDYWINE-SHOAL LIGHT-HOUSE.

BY

JOHN D. KURTZ,

LIEUT. COLONEL OF ENGINEERS, BVT. COLONEL U. S. A.;

AND

MICAH R. BROWN,

CAPTAIN OF ENGINEERS.

WASHINGTON:
GOVERNMENT PRINTING OFFICE.
1874.

ENGINEER DEPARTMENT, UNITED STATES ARMY.

REPORT

ON THE

EFFECTS OF THE SEA-WATER AND EXPOSURE

UPON THE

IRON-PILE SHAFTS

OF

THE BRANDYWINE-SHOAL LIGHT-HOUSE.

BY

JOHN D. KURTZ,

LIEUT. COLONEL OF ENGINEERS, BVT. COLONEL U. S. A.;

AND

MICAH R. BROWN,

CAPTAIN OF ENGINEERS.

WASHINGTON:
GOVERNMENT PRINTING OFFICE
1874.

OFFICE OF THE CHIEF OF ENGINEERS,
Washington, D. C., December 17, 1873.

SIR: Lieut. Col. J. D. Kurtz, Corps of Engineers, in charge of the construction of the iron-pile landing-pier at the Delaware Breakwater Harbor, has prepared a report on the effects of the sea-water and exposure upon the metal subjected to their influences at that work.

As this is a matter of interest to engineers, I have respectfully to recommend that the report be printed at the Government Printing Office, and that five hundred copies be furnished on requisition from this office.

Very respectfully, your obedient servant,

A. A. HUMPHREYS,
Brig. Gen. and Chief of Engineers.

Hon. W. W. BELKNAP,
Secretary of War.

Approved:
BY ORDER OF THE SECRETARY OF WAR:

H. T. CROSBY, *Chief Clerk.*

REPORT.

UNITED STATES ENGINEER OFFICE,
Philadelphia, Pa., December 3, 1873.

GENERAL: Since I have been on duty here, it has been several times proposed by the officers of engineers on light-house duty to examine the iron-pile shafts of the Brandywine light-house, for the purpose of ascertaining the effects of the sea-water and exposure upon the metal subjected to those influences.

The construction of the iron-pile landing-pier at the Delaware Breakwater Harbor, which I have in charge, has caused this question to become one of great interest to me, and I therefore made an arrangement with Lieut. Col. W. F. Raynolds, Corps of Engineers, light-house engineer of this district, by which he supplied a steam-tender and crew, and I furnished a party from the pier, with diver, suit, and necessary apparatus to make the examination. Capt. M. R. Brown, Corps of Engineers, in immediate charge of the construction of the pier, took personal charge of the party and directed the investigation.

The Brandywine light-house is within the mouth of Delaware Bay, and nearly nine miles from Cape May light, from which it bears about northwest by west.

The piles which support the light-house were put down in 1848, and those of the ice-fender system about it in 1849, except the outer row (38), placed in 1856 and 1857. The light-house piles are hammered iron; the fender-piles, rolled iron.

The subject is one of general interest to engineers engaged upon submarine works, and it is of special importance to the Light-House Establishment, which is engaging so largely in the use of iron piles for the substructures of light-houses.

Much discussion has been given to the question of the endurance of iron exposed to sea-water; but I have not seen any account of actual measurements, made after a number of years' exposure, of structures built of it. The present examination is, therefore, of more interest and value.

The papers which accompany this communication are as follows:

No. 1. Letter to Capt. M. R. Brown, dated July 15, 1873.

No. 2. Letter to Capt. M. R. Brown, dated July 26, 1873.

No. 3. Memorandum inclosed in No. 2.

No. 4. Report of Capt. M. R. Brown, dated August 2, 1873.

No. 5. Tabular statement accompanying No. 4.

No. 6. Diagram accompanying No. 4.

No. 6½. Plan of ice-harbor at Brandywine light-house.

No. 7. Plan of longitudinal section of ice-fender system of light-house.

No. 8. Diagram on which are platted the measurements on the pile-shafts.

No. 9. Letter of Capt. M. R. Brown, dated October 3, 1873.

Very respectfully, your obedient servant,

J. D. KURTZ,
Lieut. Col. Engineers.

Brig. Gen. A. A. HUMPHREYS,
Chief of Engineers U. S. A., Washington, D. C.

No. 1.

UNITED STATES ENGINEER OFFICE,
Philadelphia, Pa., July 15, 1873.

CAPTAIN: I have arranged with Lieutenant-Colonel Raynolds, the engineer of this district, for an examination of the iron shafts of the Brandywine light-house. He will furnish the use of his vessel, a tug of 65 feet length, and the crew of three or four men, say ordinary laborers. We are to furnish the diver, suit, and apparatus, and such skilled labor as is needed. There are probably at the light-house calipers and a scraper, but it will be safer for you to provide these and a measuring-rod. The water is about six feet deep at low tide; the distance from the Lewes pier fourteen miles, according to the chart.

The vessel will be sent to Lewes whenever you are ready for her, and can wait there for a good day. With this precaution, I think the examination may be made in one day, as two hours will suffice to steam the distance required. If more than one day is required, it will be better to return to the pier with our people for the night.

Colonel Raynolds wishes the examination to be made before the 1st of August.

Please to say when the vessel should report to you, and give me any suggestions that occur to your mind.

Very respectfully,

J. D. KURTZ,
Lieut. Col. Engineers.

Capt. M. R. Brown,
Corps of Engineers, Lewes, Del.

No. 2.

Engineer Office,
Fort Delaware, July 26, 1873.

Sir: Inclosed is a copy of a letter from Colonel Raynolds, stating that the tug will go down to Lewes for your use.

It will not be necessary for you to wait expecting Colonel Raynolds or myself. The examination of the light-house can be made whenever you are ready.

Inclosed is a memorandum of such points as occur to me respecting the examination. It is not instructions but suggestions merely. The examination will be made as you find most expedient, and as circumstances allow.

Very respectfully, your obedient servant,

J. D. KURTZ,
Lieut. Col. Engineers.

Capt. M. R. Brown,
Corps of Engineers, Lewes, Del.

No. 3.

Memorandum for Captain Brown.

In making the examination of the pile-shafts of the Brandywine light-house, the following points should be attended to:

As many of the shafts should be examined as circumstances will allow; selecting for examination those that are farthest apart.

The shaft should be scraped as carefully as practicable, and the measurements made at vertical intervals apart of about a foot with the calipers. At least two diameters (at right angles to each other, say one up and down stream and one across the current) should be taken at each interval.

If deep erosions or holes are observed, they should be specially located and measured.

The shafts have been in place about twenty-five years. When put down they were supplied with zinc collars, and these deposited zinc on the iron along a cylinder about two feet long on the shaft. If any remains of these collars or deposits exist, let them be noted.

The portions of the shafts above water should be calipered as well as those below.

If there is any disturbance or "cant" about the frame, have it noted. A mason's level will aid in determining this.

Any deposit or cutting of the bottom about the shafts should be noted, and the general condition of the iron of the superstructure.

No. 4.

UNITED STATES ENGINEER OFFICE,
Lewes, Del., August 2, 1873.

SIR: Herein I present a report of the examination of certain of the piles of the substructure of the light-house on Brandywine Shoal, Delaware Bay, and accompanying it a tabular statement of the most important results of the inspection.

On the 15th of July I received a letter from you requesting to know when I could be ready to make use of the light-house tender "Rose" for the purpose of examining as many as practicable of the piles supporting the Brandywine light-house; your letter included certain suggestions, specifying the information to be sought for.

In reply I expressed myself ready to undertake the work as soon as the "Rose" should report and the weather would allow.

The captain of the light-house tender reported to me Tuesday, July 29. All necessary tools, &c., having been prepared, arrangements were made to visit the light-house the following day; accordingly, I was awakened at 4 a. m. of Wednesday, July 30. The sky was then cloudless, and the atmosphere clear; but very soon a fog enveloped both land and water, and at 6 a. m., the hour designated for starting, the fog was quite dense, and it was not until 8 o'clock that it was thought safe to steam away. We arrived off Brandywine Shoal at 10.20 a. m., and at once transferred the working-party and apparatus to the light-house.

There was a considerable swell on the bay, which gradually lessened, however, and the sea became quite calm, considering our whereabouts.

The platform of the light-house we found was more than twenty feet from the surface of the water, and it was at once apparent that we should be compelled to work from a temporary platform which we must build on that system of horizontal braces about six feet from the surface of the water at a mean stage of the tide. Some heavy planks were found at the light-house, which were lowered and put in place as platforms to serve as a base to hold the air-pump, &c., and to admit of some little convenience in working.

Shortly after 11 o'clock we began measuring beneath the water. At 12 o'clock work was suspended for three-quarters of an hour, to enable the men to eat dinner. At 1.15 p. m. we were again measuring under water, and work was continued until 6 p. m., when we prepared to return to the "Rose." We were aboard and steaming toward Lewes at 6.45, reaching the railroad-pier at 9 p. m.

Thus far only six piles had been examined, and one of these somewhat imperfectly. Not having much previous knowledge of the light-house, I had somewhat underrated the scope and difficulty of the work involved in a thorough examination of the structure. The whole number of piles in the substructure is seventy-seven, and nearly all are covered with considerable metamorphosed iron, difficult in most cases to scrape off, and many with coral and other adhering substances, which add to the difficulty. The current here is quite strong, and around the piles is broken into numerous eddies. The water is about nine feet deep at low water.

The lower horizontal system of braces, at about the plane of low water, have in many localities dropped to the bottom; the cast-iron collars which held them having been broken apparently by the weight of superincumbent ice, and the momentum of masses of such ice acted on by the waves. In this way, the lower system of braces is almost completely gone on the northern side to an east and west line, just south of the north pile of the main structure (of 1848). They are also gone in the center of the southern half of the octagon. Occasional braces of the same system, about one-third of the original number, are out of place in the south end of the fender system; and, in fact, so few remain throughout the whole structure in this lower system that it is practically nearly useless, since the remainder are bent downward in various planes, as though by a heavy weight or violent impact, and they appear nearly ready to follow those that have sunk. These latter being supported just above the bottom by remnants of collars, it is difficult for a diver to walk about in a current so strong; and considerable time being required to move our temporary platform from one locality to another, it became apparent that we must measure groups of piles sufficiently near to each other to necessitate few changes of the platform, in order to obtain enough results to be of much value in an inspection as limited in time as this was.

Having fallen so far short of previous anticipations in our first day's work, I resolved to return again on the following day, if practicable. Accordingly, at 6.20 a. m., July 31, we were on our way to the light-house, which we reached with our apparatus at 9 a. m. At 10 o'clock we began measuring beneath the water's surface. Lunch was this time sent to the men from the light-house tender. The platform was twice removed this day. The work continued until 4.45 p. m., when we started on our return to Lewes, reaching the railroad-pier at 6.10 p. m.

This day we measured six piles; one of these had been unsatisfactorily examined the previous day. Several characteristic braces were measured also, as will be seen by the table.

I judge that a thorough examination of the entire structure would consume two or three weeks of fair weather, and would probably yield results of considerable value and interest.

All the piles are more or less perceptibly wanting in verticality, but very few of them seriously so; the two most remarkably inclined abnormally are marked X and Y on the accompanying diagram. They are so bent above water as to be inclined about 15° and 10° respectively to the vertical.

No great departure from a horizontal plane is noticeable in the platform of the light-house, but apparently the southeast portion over the pile X is slightly inclined downward to the southeast.

The light-house itself exhibits nothing abnormal; many of the diagonal braces, in vertical planes, far above the surface of the water, are so peculiarly corroded as to resemble (on the exterior) in a striking degree the bark of a red-oak tree, with deep seams and scales.

Ten zinc collars are still visible above low-water mark on as many piles, mainly of the fender-structure. No evidences appear that any one of the piles has become coated with zinc, however, even in a slight degree.

The notes on the accompanying diagram and the tables seem to indicate all else not included in the body of this report, which your instructions and my limited opportunities appear to call for in this paper.

Very respectfully, your obedient servant,

M. R. BROWN,
Capt. Engineers, U. S. A.

Lieut. Col. J. D. KURTZ,
Corps of Engineers, U. S. A.,
Philadelphia, Pa.

Remarks.

The piles examined are denoted by numbers and letters, except the center-pile, which is so designated, and are tabulated in the order in which the examinations were made.

The numbers refer to the piles of the light-house proper, and the letters to those of the fender-system.

All adhering substances as well as the oxidized iron were removed before the measurements were taken.

Where breaks occur in the table, it was for some reason impracticable to measure at those places.

Thirteen of the sixteen vertical diagonal braces of round iron and six of the sixteen horizontal square iron braces were measured.

Center-pile.—Diver reported a hole about two feet deep, lined with stones, in the bed around the pile on the south side, and a corresponding elevation of sand and stones on the north side. The pile was covered with barnacles and a soft substance, enlarging its diameter about half an inch.

No. 6.—Small measurements result from erosion, long seams of one or two feet in length; this pile is also badly pitted or pockmarked. Bottom, stones and no sand, nearly level.

No. 7.—Has grooves about five inches long, and deep enough to bury the thumb; it is also bent twice, a reverse curve.

No. 8.—The lower collar on this pile has dropped down, and is about one foot and a half from the bottom.

A.—Small measurements are erosion.

B.—Sand bottom, no rust on pile, but covered with hard, coral-like substance.

C.—Diver reports a hole one foot and a half from bottom, about two inches deep, and one inch in diameter, nearly circular; another three feet and a half from bottom, about four inches long, one inch and a half deep and wide; from this a crack extends upward two feet, and is about two inches deep.

D.—This pile and others of the outer series covered on the northeast side with coral.

M. R. BROWN,
Capt. Engineers, U. S. A.

No. 9.

UNITED STATES ENGINEER OFFICE,
Lewes, Del., October 3, 1873.

SIR: * * * * * * * *

Referring to the direction in which measurements of the diameters of the piles of the Brandywine Light-house were made, in my recent examination, ("North and south") and ("East and west") mean, as nearly as could be judged, in the direction of the longest axis of the whole structural arrangement of piles for the first ("North and south"), and at right angles or in the direction of the shortest axis for the second ("East and west"). We had no means of ascertaining exactly the direction of the cardinal points, but it was easy to see that the long axis of the work was nearly in a meridian.

Concerning the average direction of the current, I had no means of knowing it accurately; but as well as I could tell from two days' observation, it did not diverge more than 15° from the long axis. I cannot but think that either the salient angles of the light-house were placed originally in the direction of strong currents, or that the same reason, if any, which induced its constructors to set its long axis at an angle with the current applied with equal force to the determination of the choice of planes in which to measure the diameters.

It would have been impracticable to do accurate work in any other directions than those we chose. The braces were a better guide for the diver than anything else, and they run mainly north and south, and east and west.

Very respectfully, your obedient servant,

M. R. BROWN,
Capt. Engineers, U. S. A.

Lieut. Col. J. D. KURTZ,
Corps of Engineers, U. S. A., Philadelphia, Pa.

○

No. 5.—(To accompany report of August 2, 1873.)

Results of the examination of the substructure of the screw-pile light-house on Brandywine Shoal.—Dates of examination, July 30 and 31, 1873.

DIAMETERS OF PILES.

Distance from bottom, in feet	CENTER-PILE. North and south.	Mean.	East and west.	Mean.	Mean of means.	No. 6. North and south.	Mean.	East and west.	Mean.	Mean of means.
	Inches.	*Inches.*	*Inches.*	*Inches.*	*Inches.*	*Inches.*	*Inches.*	*Inches.*	*Inches.*	*Inches.*
0										
1	5 7-8					6 1-16		4 7-8		5 15-32
2	6					5 7-16		5 1-8		5 9-32
3	5 7-8					5 5-8		5 3-16		5 13-32
4	5 1-2					5 9-16		5 1-2		5 19-32
5	5 7-16					5 13-16		5 9-16		5 11-16
6	5 7-16					4 5-8		5 5-16		5 15-32
7										
8	5 1-2		5 1-2		5 1-2					
9	5 9-16		5 17-32		5 35-64					
10	5 5-8		5 1-2		5 9-16					
11	5 5-8		5 9-16		5 19-32					
12	5 19-32		5 9-16		5 37-64					
13	5 1-2		5 1-2		5 1-2					
14	5 7-16		5 3-8		5 13-32					
15										
16										

Distance from bottom, in feet	No. 7. North and south.	Mean.	East and west.	Mean.	Mean of means.	No. 3. North and south.	Mean.	East and west.	Mean.	Mean of means.
	Inches.	*Inches.*	*Inches.*	*Inches.*	*Inches.*	*Inches.*	*Inches.*	*Inches.*	*Inches.*	*Inches.*
0										
1	5 3-4		5 7-8		5 13-16					
2	5 3-8		5 3-8		5 3-8					
3	5 3-4		6		5 7-8					
4	5 3-4		5 7-16		5 19-32					
5	5 11-16		5 3-8		5 17-32					
6	5 3-8		5 3-8		5 3-8					
7	5 9-16		5 3-16		5 3-8					
8	5 7-16		5 3-8		5 13-32	5 7-16		5 7-16		5 7-16
9	5 1-2		5 7-16		5 15-32	5 3-8		5 7-16		5 13-32
10	5 1-2		5 1-2		5 1-2	5 3-8		5 1-2		5 7-16
11	5 1-2		5 7-16		5 15-32	5 7-16		5 1-2		5 15-32
12	5 1-2		5 7-16		5 15-32	5 7-16		5 1-2		5 15-32
13	5 7-16		5 1-2		5 15-32	5 1-2		5 7-16		5 15-32
14						5 9-16		5 9-16		5 9-16
15										
16										

Distance from bottom, in feet	No. 5. North and south.	Mean.	East and west.	Mean.	Mean of means.	No. 8. North and south.	Mean.	East and west.	Mean.	Mean of means.
	Inches.	*Inches.*	*Inches.*	*Inches.*	*Inches.*	*Inches.*	*Inches.*	*Inches.*	*Inches.*	*Inches.*
0								6 1-8, 6 1-16	6 3-32	
1						5 5-8				
2						5 5-8		*a* 5 3-4		
3						5 9-16		*b* 5 5-8		
4						5 5-8		6, 5 5-8	5 13-16	5 23-32
5						5 3-8		5 1-4		5 5-16
6								5 3-8		
7										
8	5 7-16		5 7-16			5 7-16		5 1-2		5 15-32
9	5 3-4		5 7-16		5 19-32	5 1-2		5 1-2		5 1-2
10	5 7-8		6		5 15-16	5 9-16		5 1-2		5 19-32
11	5 1-2		5 7-8		5 11-16	5 9-16		5 1-2		5 19-32
12	5 1-2		5 1-2		5 1-2	5 9-16		5 1-2		5 19-32
13	5 17-32		5 1-2		5 23-64	5 1-2		5 9-16		5 19-32
14	5 17-32		5 1-2		5 23-64	5 1-2		5 1-2		5 1-2
15										
16										

Distance from bottom, in feet	A. North and south.	Mean.	East and west.	Mean.	Mean of means.	B. North and south.	Mean.	East and west.	Mean.	Mean of means.
0	5 7-16		5 7-16		5 7-16	5 3-4		5 5-8		5 11-16
1	5 1-8		5 1-32		5 5-64	5 5-8		5 7-16		5 17-32
2	5 5-16		5 1-2, 5 1-4	5 3-8	5 11-16	5 11-16		5 5-8		5 21-32
3	5 5-16		5 3-32		5 5-64	5 3-8		5 7-16		5 13-32
4	4 15-16, 5 3-32	5 1-64	4 3-4		4 113-128	5 13-16, 4 17-32	5 11-64	5 19-32 5 5-16		5 49-128
5	4 7-8		5 1-16		4 31-32	5 17-32		5 9-16		5 35-64
6	4 13-16		4 3-4		4 25-32	5 1-2		5 1-2		5 1-2
7										
8										
9						5 5-16		5 3-8		5 11-32
10	5 1-16		5		5 1-32	5 1-2		5 1-2		5 1-2
11	5 +		5 1-16		5 1-32	5 1-2		5 1-2		5 1-2
12	5 +		5		5 +	5 1-2		5 1-2		5 1-2
13	5 +		5		5 +	5 9-16		5 1-2		5 19-32
14	5		5		5	5 9-16		5 1-2 +		5 19-32
15	5 +		5		5 +	Too rusty to	measure			

Distance from bottom, in feet	No. 1. North and south.	Mean.	East and west.	Mean.	Mean of means.	C. North and south.	Mean.	East and west.	Mean.	Mean of means.
0						5 1-8		5 7-8		5 1-2
1	5 13-16		6 1-8		5 31-32	4 3-16, 4 13-16	4 1-2	5		4 3-4
2	5 13-16		6 5-8		6 7-32	4 15-16, 4 7-8	4 47-64	4 15-16, 4 7-8	4 29-32	4 105-128
3	6 3-8		6 3-4		6 1-2	5 7-16		5 7-16		5 7-16
4	5 9-16 5 1-2		5 11-16		5 5-8	4 3-4, 4 15-16, 5 1-8	4 15-16	4 15-16		4 15-16
5	5 7-8		5 7-8		5 7-8	5 1-16		5 1-16		5 1-16
6	5 7-16		5 9-32		5 23-64	4 9-16		5		4 25-32
7	6		5 7-8		5 15-16					
8										
9	5 9-16		5 9-16		5 9-16					
10	5 9-16		5 9-16		5 9-16	5 3-16		5 3-16		5 3-16
11	5 1-2		5 9-16		5 19-32	5		5 1-16		5 1-32
12	5 1-2		5 9-16		5 19-32	5		4 15-16		4 31-32
13	5 1-2		5 9-16		5 19-32	5 1-16		4 15-16		5
14	5 1-2		5 5-8		5 9-16	5 1-16		4 15-16		5
15	5 3-8		5 1-2		5 7-16	5 1-16		4 15-16		5

Distance from bottom, in feet	D. North and south.	Mean.	East and west.	Mean.	Mean of means.
0	5 13-16		6		5 29-32
1	5 11-32		5 1-2		5 27-64
2	5 3-4		5 7-8		5 13-16
3	5 13-32		5 9-16		5 21-64
4	6 1-32, 5 11-16, 5 5-8	5 26-32	5 13-16		5 26-32
5	5 3-4		5 19-32		5 43-64
6	5 9-16		5 9-16		5 9-16
7	5 1-2		5 13-32		5 29-64
8					
9	5 7-16		5 1-2		5 15-32
10	5 7-16		5 1-2		5 15-32
11	5 7-16		5 1-2		5 15-32
12	5 7-16		5 3-8		5 13-32
13	5 1-2		5 7-16		5 15-22
14	5 9-16		5 7-16		5 1-2
15	5 3-4 over rust.		5 3-4 over	rust	5 3-4

Vertical diagonal braces, round.

Inches.	*Inches.*	*Inches.*
1 7-16	1 1-2	1 1-2
1 1-2	1 7-16	1 7-16
1 1-2	1 7-16	1 7-16
1 7-16	1 7-16	
1 7-16	1 1-2	

Horizontal braces, square.

Inches.	*Inches.*	*Means.*
2 7-8	2 13-16	2 27-32
2 13-16	2 13-16	2 13-16
2 7-8	2 7-8	2 7-8
2 13-16	2 13-16	2 13-16
2 7-8	2 7-8	2 7-8
2 13-16	2 7-8	2 27-32

a At 1 1-2 feet. *b* At 3 1-2 feet.

No. 6.

Diagram of Brandywine Light House, at Plane of upper horizontal braces.

Note. The 4 centre piles of the fender system, are stump piles and do not extend above the plane of the braces.

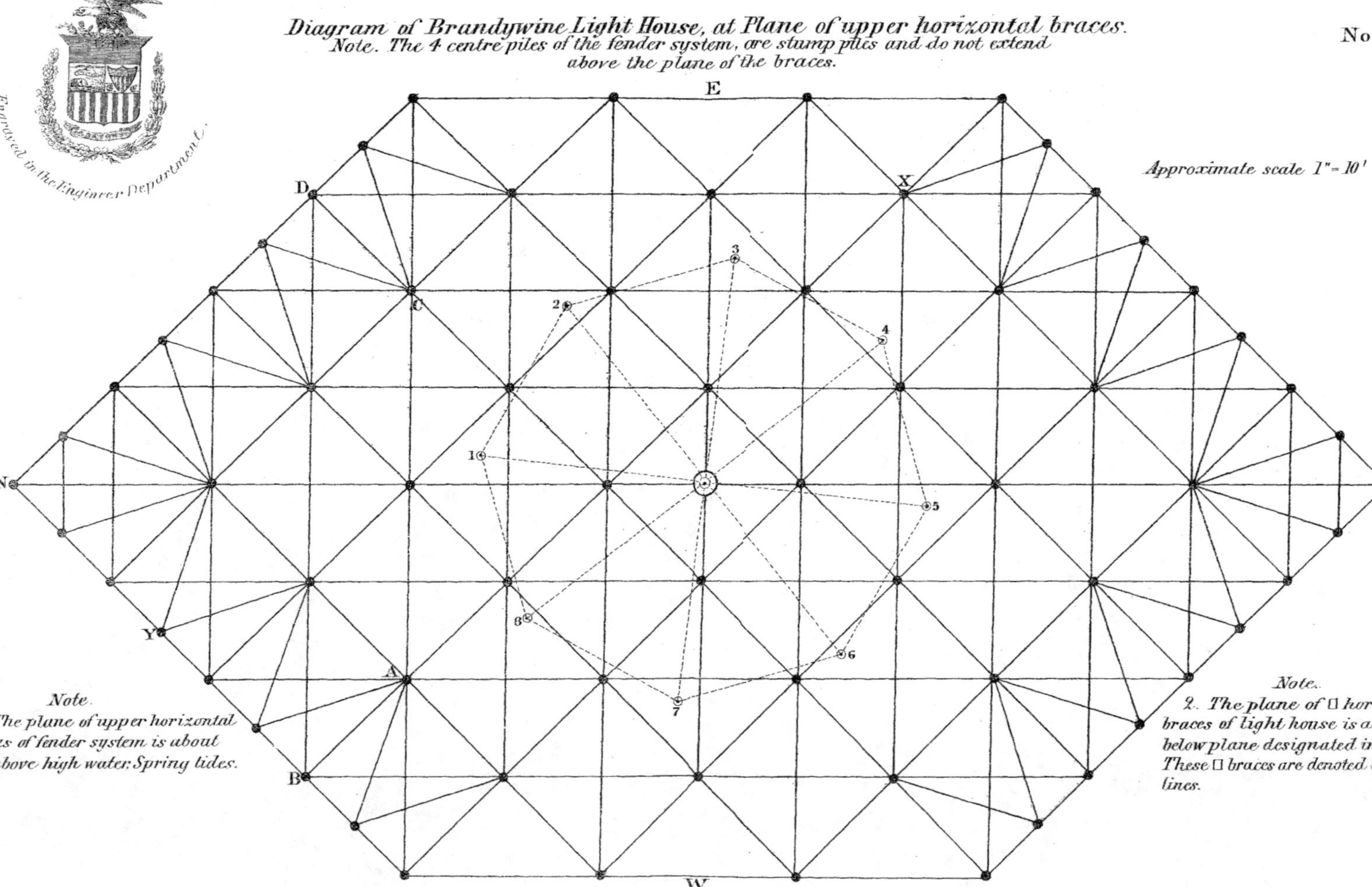

Note.

1. The plane of upper horizontal braces of fender system is about 2'6" above high water. Spring tides.

Note.

2. The plane of □ horizontal braces of light house is about 1 ft. below plane designated in Note 1. These □ braces are denoted by dotted lines.

No. 6½.

Plan of Ice Harbor at Brandywine Lighthouse

The additions are shaded.

Scale $\frac{1}{96}$, or $\frac{1}{8}''$ = 1 ft.

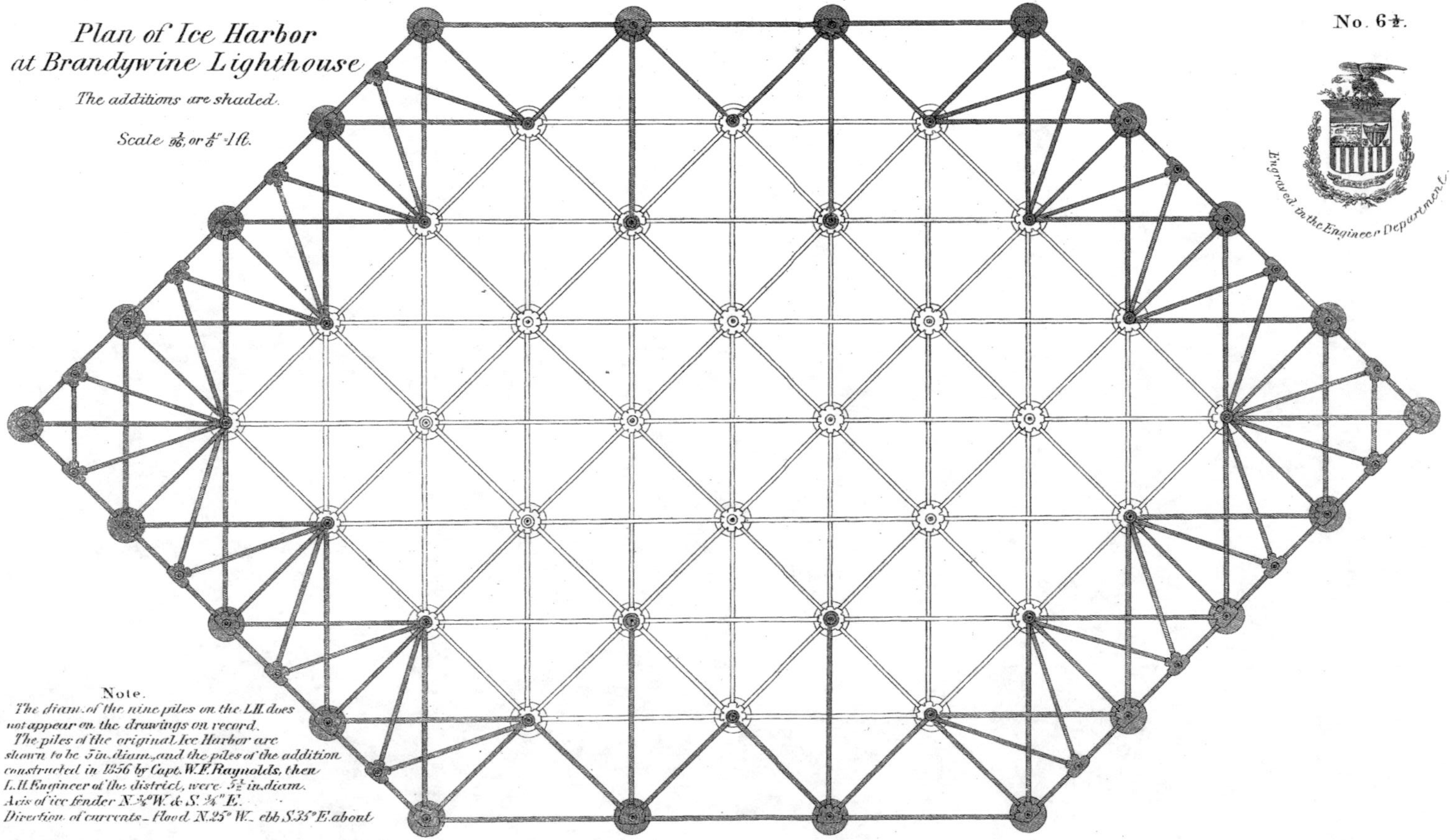

Engraved in the Engineer Department.

Note.

The diam. of the nine piles on the L.H. does not appear on the drawings on record.

The piles of the original Ice Harbor are shown to be 5 in. diam., and the piles of the addition constructed in 1856 by Capt. W. F. Raynolds, then L.H. Engineer of the district, were $5\frac{1}{2}$ in. diam.

Axis of ice fender N. ¾° W. & S. ¾° E.

Direction of currents – flood N. 25° W. – ebb S. 35° E. about

No. 7.

Longitudinal Section.

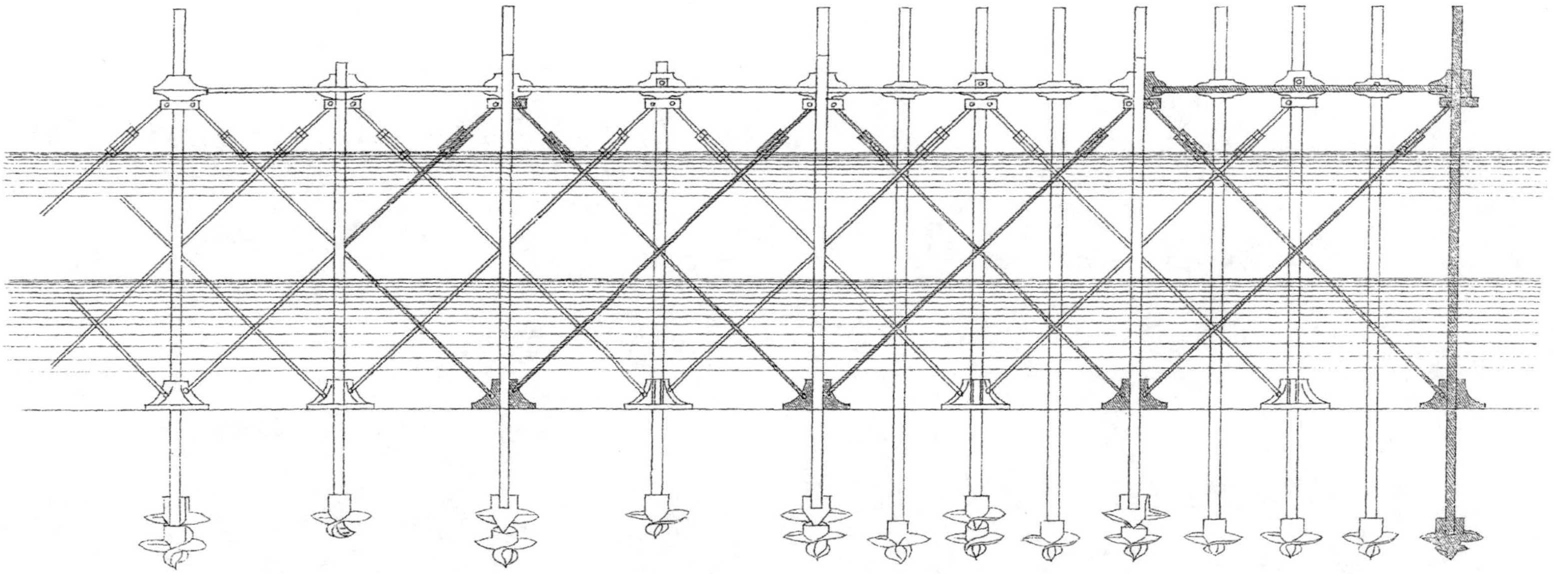

The additions are shaded.

No. 8.

DIAGRAM

of Measurements of Pile Shafts of

BRANDYWINE LIGHT-HOUSE STRUCTURE.

July, 1873.

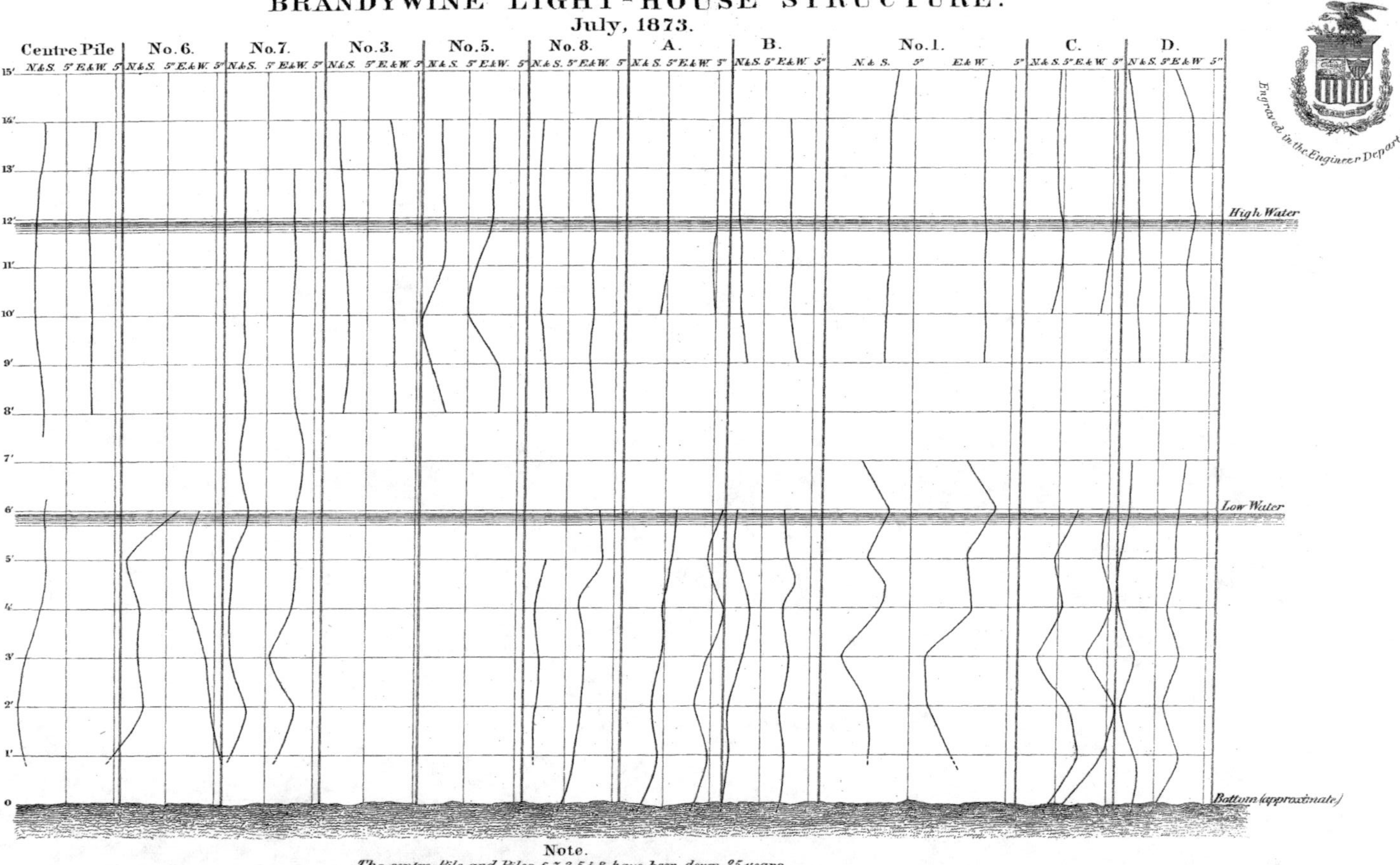

Note.

The centre Pile and Piles 6, 7, 3, 5 & 8 have been down 25 years.
Piles A & C .... " .... " .... " .... 24 .... "
" B & D .... " .... " .... " .... 16 & 17 .... "
Directions of ebb and flood currents about S. 35° E & N. 25° W.
Piles A, B, C, & D, are rolled iron, the others hammered iron.
The fine vertical lines correspond to diameters of 5 inches.
The variations (generally in excess) are shown by the heavy waved lines.
The horizontal exaggeration is twelve fold.

www.ingramcontent.com/pod-product-compliance
Lightning Source LLC
LaVergne TN
LVHW011144110826
845150LV00008B/2509

* 9 7 8 1 4 1 8 1 9 2 7 7 8 *